The Keto Guide to Air Fryer Desserts

Delicious and Healthy Recipes to Improve Your Guide and Boost Your Metabolism

America Keto Recipes

Table of Contents

1.Cinnamon Carrot Cake

Prep Time 10 m | **Cook Time** 25 m | 4 **Servings**

- 1Egg
- 1/2 teaspoon Vanilla
- 1/2 teaspoon Cinnamon
- 1/2 cup Sugar
- 1/4 cup Canola oil
- 1/4, chopped Walnuts
- 1/2 teaspoon Baking powder
- 1/2 cup Flour
- 1/4 cup Grated carrot

1.Sprinkle a baking dish with cooking spray and set aside. In a mixing bowl, beat sugar and oil for 1-2 minutes. Add vanilla, cinnamon, and egg and beat for 30 seconds. Add remaining ingredients and stir to combine. Pour batter into the prepared baking dish. Place steam rack into the instant pot. Place baking dish on top of the steam rack. Seal pot with the air fryer lid. Select bake mode and cook at 350 F for 25 minutes. Serve.

Per Serving: Calories 340 Carbs 39g Fat 19g Protein 5g

2.Blueberry Muffins

Prep Time 15 m | **Cook Time** 20 m | 6 **Servings**

- 2 Eggs
- 1 1/2 cups Blueberries
- 1 cup Yogurt
- 1 cup Sugar
- 1 tablespoon Baking powder
- 2 cups Flour
- 2 teaspoons fresh lemon juice
- 2 tablespoons, grated Lemon zest
- 1 teaspoon Vanilla
- 1/2 cup Oil
- 1/2 teaspoon Salt

1.Using a small bowl, mix flour, salt, and baking powder. Set aside. In a large bowl, whisk together eggs, lemon juice, lemon zest, vanilla, oil, yogurt, and sugar. Add flour mixture and blueberries into the egg mixture and fold well. Pour batter into 9 silicone muffin molds. Place the dehydrating tray into the multi-level air fryer basket and place the basket into the instant pot. Place 6 muffin molds on the dehydrating tray. Seal pot with the air fryer lid. Select bake mode and cook at 375 F for 20 minutes. Cook remaining muffins. Serve.

Per Serving: Calories 343 Carbs 50g Fat 13g Protein 5.9g

3.Almond Raspberry Muffins

Prep Time 10 m | **Cook Time** 35 m | 6 **Servings**

- 2 Eggs
- 1 teaspoon Baking powder
- 5 ounces Almond meal
- 2 tablespoons Coconut oil
- 2 tablespoons Honey
- 3 ounces Raspberries

1.In a bowl, mix almond meal and baking powder. Add honey, eggs, and oil and stir until thoroughly combined. Add raspberries and fold well. Pour batter into the 6-silicone muffin molds. Place the dehydrating tray into the multi-level air fryer basket and place the basket into the instant pot. Place 6 muffin molds on the dehydrating tray. Seal pot with the air fryer lid. Select bake mode and cook at 350 F for 35 minutes. Serve.

Per Serving: Calories 227 Carbs 13g Fat 17g Protein 7g

4.Chocolate Butter Cake

Prep time: 20 m | **Cook time:** 11 m | **Serves:** 4

- 4 ounces (113 g) butter, melted
- 4 ounces (113 g) dark chocolate
- 2 eggs, lightly whisked
- 2 tablespoons monk fruit
- 2 tablespoons almond meal
- 1 teaspoon baking powder
- ½ teaspoon ground cinnamon ¼ teaspoon ground star anise

1. Begin by preheating your Air Fryer to 370 degrees F (188ºC). Spritz the sides and bottom of a baking pan with nonstick cooking spray.
2. Melt the butter and dark chocolate in a microwave-safe bowl. Mix the eggs and monk fruit until frothy.
3. Pour the butter/chocolate mixture into the egg mixture. Stir in the almond meal, baking powder, cinnamon, and star anise. Mix until everything is well incorporated.
4. Scrape the batter into the prepared pan. Bake in the preheated Air Fryer for 9 to 11 minutes.
5. Let stand for 2 minutes. Invert on a plate while warm and serve.

Per Serving: calories: 408 | fat: 39g | protein: 8g | carbs: 7g | net carbs: 3g | fiber: 4g

5.Buttery Chocolate Cake

Prep time: 20 m | **Cook time:**11 m | **Serves:** 4

- 2½ ounces (71 g) butter, at room temperature 3 ounces (85 g) chocolate, unsweetened 2 eggs, beaten
- ½ cup Swerve
- ½ cup almond flour
- 1 teaspoon rum extract
- 1 teaspoon vanilla extract

1. Begin by preheating your Air Fryer to 370 degrees F (188ºC). Spritz the sides and bottom of four ramekins with cooking spray.
2. Melt the butter and chocolate in a microwave-safe bowl. Mix the eggs and Swerve until frothy.
3. Pour the butter/chocolate mixture into the egg mixture. Stir in the almond flour, rum extract, and vanilla extract. Mix until everything is well incorporated.
4. Scrape the batter into the prepared ramekins. Bake in the preheated Air Fryer for 9 to 11 minutes.
5. Let stand for 2 to 3 minutes. Invert on a plate while warm and serve. Bon appétit!

Per Serving: calories: 364 | fat: 33g | protein: 8g | carbs: 9g | net carbs: 4g | fiber: 5g

6.Chocolate Butter Cake

Prep Time:30 m | **Cook time:**22 m | **Serves:** 10

- 1 cup no-sugar-added peanut butter
- 1¼ cups monk fruit
- 3 eggs
- 1 cup almond flour
- 1 teaspoon baking powder
- ¼ teaspoon kosher salt
- 1 cup unsweetened bakers' chocolate, broken into chunks

1. Start by preheating your Air Fryer to 350 degrees F (180ºC). Now, spritz the sides and bottom of a baking pan with cooking spray.
2. In a mixing dish, thoroughly combine the peanut butter with the monk fruit until creamy. Next, fold in the egg and beat until fluffy.
3. After that, stir in the almond flour, baking powder, salt, and baker's chocolate. Mix until everything is well combined.
4. Bake in the preheated Air Fryer for 20 to 22 minutes. Transfer to a wire rack to cool before slicing and serving.

Per Serving: calories: 207 | fat: 17g | protein: 8g | carbs: 6g | net carbs: 3g | fiber: 3g

7.Butter Chocolate Cake with Pecan

Prep Time:30 m | **Cook time:**22 m | **Serves:** 6

- ½ cup butter, melted
- ½ cup Swerve
- 1 teaspoon vanilla essence
- 1 egg
- ½   cup almond flour
- ½   teaspoon baking powder ¼ cup cocoa powder
- ½   teaspoon ground cinnamon ¼ teaspoon fine sea salt
- 1 ounce (28 g) bakers' chocolate, unsweetened ¼ cup pecans, finely chopped

1. Start by preheating your Air Fryer to 350 degrees F (180ºC). Now, lightly grease six silicone molds.
2. In a mixing dish, beat the melted butter with the Swerve until fluffy. Next, stir in the vanilla and egg and beat again.
3. After that, add the almond flour, baking powder, cocoa powder, cinnamon, and salt. Mix until everything is well combined.
4. Fold in the chocolate and pecans; mix to combine. Bake in the preheated Air Fryer for 20 to 22 minutes.

Per Serving: calories: 253 | fat: 25g | protein: 4g | carbs: 6g | net carbs: 3g | fiber: 3g

8.Baked Cheesecake

Prep Time:40 m | **Cook time:**35 m | **Serves:** 6

- ½ cup almond flour
- 1½ tablespoons unsalted butter, melted
- 2 tablespoons erythritol
- 1 (8-ounce / 227-g) package cream cheese, softened
- ¼ cup powdered erythritol ½ teaspoon vanilla paste
- 1 egg, at room temperature

Topping:

- 1½ cups sour cream
- 3 tablespoons powdered erythritol
- 1 teaspoon vanilla extract

1. Thoroughly combine the almond flour, butter, and 2 tablespoons of erythritol in a mixing bowl. Press the mixture into the bottom of lightly greased custard cups.
2. Then, mix the cream cheese, ¼ cup of powdered erythritol, vanilla, and egg using an electric mixer at low speed. Pour the batter into the pan, covering the crust.
3. Bake in the preheated Air Fryer at 330 degrees F (166ºC) for 35 minutes until edges are puffed and the surface is firm.
4. Mix the sour cream, 3 tablespoons of powdered erythritol, and vanilla for the topping; spread over the crust and allow it to cool to room temperature.
5. Transfer to your refrigerator for 6 to 8 hours.

Per Serving: calories: 306 | fat: 27g | protein: 8g | carbs: 9g | net carbs: 7g | fiber: 2g

9.Crusted Mini Cheesecake

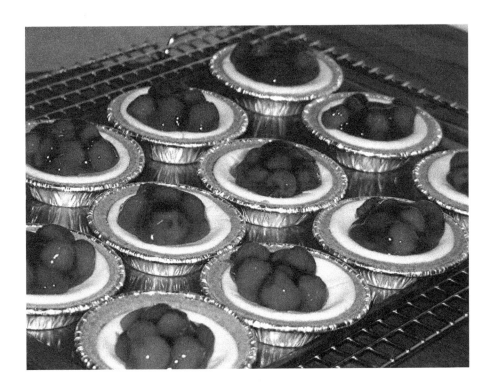

Prep Time:30 m | **Cook time:**18 m | **Serves:** 8

For the Crust:
- ⅓ teaspoon grated nutmeg
- 1½ tablespoons erythritol
- 1½ cups almond meal
- 8 tablespoons melted butter
- 1 teaspoon ground cinnamon
- A pinch of kosher salt, to taste

For the Cheesecake:
- 2 eggs
- ½ cups unsweetened chocolate chips 1½ tablespoons sour cream
- 4 ounces (113 g) soft cheese
- ½ cup Swerve
- ½ teaspoon vanilla essence

1. Firstly, line eight cups of a mini muffin pan with paper liners.
2. To make the crust, mix the almond meal with erythritol, cinnamon, nutmeg, and kosher salt.
3. Now, add melted butter and stir well to moisten the crumb mixture.
4. Divide the crust mixture among the muffin cups and press gently to make even layers.
5. In another bowl, whip together the soft cheese, sour cream, and Swerve until uniform and smooth. Fold in the eggs and the vanilla essence.
6. Then, divide chocolate chips among the prepared muffin cups. Then, add the cheese mix to each muffin cup.
7. Bake for about 18 minutes at 345 degrees F (174ºC). Bake in batches if needed. To finish, transfer the mini cheesecakes to a cooling rack; store them in the fridge.

Per Serving: calories: 314 | fat: 29g | protein: 7g | carbs: 7g | net carbs: 4g | fiber: 3g

10.Creamy Cheese Cake

Prep Time:1 h | **Cook time:**37 m | **Serves:** 8

- 1½ cups almond flour
- 3 ounces (85 g) Swerve
- ½ stick butter, melted
- 20 ounces (567 g) full-fat cream cheese
- ½ cup heavy cream
- 1¼ cups granulated Swerve
- 3 eggs, at room temperature
- 1 tablespoon vanilla essence
- 1 teaspoon grated lemon zest

1. Coat the sides and bottom of a baking pan with a little flour.
2. In a mixing bowl, combine the almond flour and Swerve. Add the melted butter and mix until your mixture looks like bread crumbs.
3. Press the mixture into the bottom of the prepared pan to form an even layer. Bake at 330 degrees F (166ºC) for 7 minutes until golden brown. Allow it to cool completely on a wire rack.
4. Meanwhile, in a mixer fitted with the paddle attachment, prepare the filling by mixing the soft cheese, heavy cream, and granulated Swerve; beat until creamy and fluffy.
5. Crack the eggs into the mixing bowl, one at a time; add the vanilla and lemon zest and continue to mix until fully combined.
6. Pour the prepared topping over the cooled crust and spread evenly.
7. Bake in the preheated Air Fryer at 330 degrees F (166ºC) for 25 to 30 minutes; leave it in the Air Fryer to keep warm for another 30 minutes.

8. Cover your cheesecake with plastic wrap. Place in your refrigerator and allow it to cool at least 6 hours or overnight. Serve well chilled.

Per Serving: calories: 245 | fat: 21g | protein: 8g | carbs: 7g | net carbs: 5g | fiber: 2g

11.Air Fried Chocolate Brownies

Prep Time:40 m | **Cook time:**35 m | **Serves:** 8

- 5 ounces (142 g) unsweetened chocolate, chopped into chunks
- 2 tablespoons instant espresso powder
- 1 tablespoon cocoa powder, unsweetened
- ½ cup almond butter
- ½ cup almond meal ¾ cup Swerve
- 1 teaspoon pure coffee extract
- ½ teaspoon lime peel zest
- ¼ cup coconut flour
- 2 eggs plus 1 egg yolk ½ teaspoon baking soda ½ teaspoon baking powder
- ½ teaspoon ground cinnamon 1/3 teaspoon ancho chile powder

For the Chocolate Mascarpone Frosting:
- 4 ounces (113 g) mascarpone cheese, at room temperature 1½ ounces (43 g) unsweetened chocolate chips 1½ cups Swerve
- ¼ cup unsalted butter, at room temperature
- 1 teaspoon vanilla paste A pinch of fine sea salt

1. First of all, microwave the chocolate and almond butter until completely melted; allow the mixture to cool at room temperature.
2. Then, whisk the eggs, Swerve, cinnamon, espresso powder, coffee extract, ancho chile powder, and lime zest.
3. Next step, add the vanilla/egg mixture to the chocolate/butter mixture. Stir in the almond meal and coconut flour along with baking soda, baking powder, and cocoa powder.
4. Finally, press the batter into a lightly buttered cake pan. Air-fry for 35 minutes at 345 degrees F (174ºC).

5. In the meantime, make the frosting. Beat the butter and mascarpone cheese until creamy. Add in the melted chocolate chips and vanilla paste.

6. Gradually, stir in the Swerve and salt; beat until everything's well combined. Lastly, frost the brownies and serve.

Per Serving: calories: 363 | fat: 33g | protein: 7g | carbs: 10g | net carbs: 5g | fiber: 5g

12.Butter Cake with Cranberries

Prep Time:30 m | **Cook time:**20 m | **Serves:** 8

- 1 cup almond flour
- $1/3$ teaspoon baking soda
- $1/3$ teaspoon baking powder
- ¾ cup erythritol
- ½ teaspoon ground cloves
- $1/3$ teaspoon ground cinnamon
- ½ teaspoon cardamom
- 1 stick butter
- ½ teaspoon vanilla paste
- 2 eggs plus 1 egg yolk, beaten
- ½ cup cranberries, fresh or thawed
- 1 tablespoon browned butter

For Ricotta Frosting:
- ½ stick butter
- ½ cup firm Ricotta cheese
- 1 cup powdered erythritol ¼ teaspoon salt
- Zest of ½ lemon

1. Start by preheating your Air Fryer to 355 degrees F (181ºC).
2. Combine the flour with baking soda, baking powder, erythritol, ground cloves, cinnamon, and cardamom in a mixing bowl.
3. In a separate bowl, whisk 1 stick butter with vanilla paste; mix in the eggs until light and fluffy. Add the flour/sugar mixture to the butter/egg mixture. Fold in the cranberries and browned butter.
4. Scrape the mixture into the greased cake pan. Then, bake in the preheated Air Fryer for about 20 minutes.
5. Meanwhile, in a food processor, whip ½ stick of the butter and Ricotta cheese until there are no lumps.
6. Slowly add the powdered erythritol and salt until your mixture has reached a thick consistency. Stir in the

lemon zest; mix to combine and chill completely before using.

Per Serving: calories: 286 | fat: 27g | protein: 8g | carbs: 10g | net carbs: 5g | fiber: 5g

13.Buttery Monk Fruit Cookie

Prep time: 25 m | **Cook time:**20 m | **Serves:** 4

- 8 ounces (227 g) almond meal
- 2 tablespoons flaxseed meal
- 1 ounce (28 g) monk fruit
- 1 teaspoon baking powder
- A pinch of grated nutmeg
- A pinch of coarse salt
- 1 large egg, room temperature.
- 1 stick butter, room temperature
- 1 teaspoon vanilla extract

1. Mix the almond meal, flaxseed meal, monk fruit, baking powder, grated nutmeg, and salt in a bowl.
2. In a separate bowl, whisk the egg, butter, and vanilla extract.
3. Stir the egg mixture into a dry mixture; mix to combine well or until it forms a nice, soft dough.
4. Roll your dough out and cut out with a cookie cutter of your choice.
5. Bake in the preheated Air Fryer at 350 degrees F (180ºC) for 10 minutes. Decrease the temperature to 330 degrees F (166ºC) and cook for 10 minutes longer. Bon appétit!

Per Serving: calories: 388 | fat: 38g | protein: 8g | carbs: 7g | net carbs: 4g | fiber: 3g

14.Buttery Cookie with Hazelnut

Prep Time: 20 m | **Cook time:** 10 m | **Serves:** 6

- 1 cup almond flour
- ½ cup coconut flour
- 1 teaspoon baking soda
- 1 teaspoon fine sea salt
- 1 stick butter
- 1 cup Swerve
- 2 teaspoons vanilla
- 2 eggs, at room temperature
- 1 cup hazelnuts, coarsely chopped

1. Begin by preheating your Air Fryer to 350 degrees.
2. Mix the flour with baking soda and sea salt.
3. In the bowl of an electric mixer, beat the butter, Swerve, and vanilla until creamy. Fold in the eggs, one at a time, and mix until well combined.
4. Slowly and gradually stir in the flour mixture. Finally, fold in the coarsely chopped hazelnuts.
5. Divide the dough into small balls using a large cookie scoop; drop onto the prepared cookie sheets. Bake for 10 minutes or until golden brown, rotating the pan once or twice through cooking.
6. Work in batches and cool for a couple of minutes before removing to wire racks. Enjoy!

Per Serving: calories: 328 | fat: 32g | protein: 7g | carbs: 5g | net carbs: 3g | fiber: 2g

15.Hazelnut Butter Cookie

Prep Time:1 h | **Cook time:**20 m | **Serves:** 10

- 4 tablespoons liquid monk fruit
- ½ cup hazelnuts, ground
- 1 stick butter, room temperature
- 2 cups almond flour
- 1 cup coconut flour
- 2 ounces (57 g) granulated Swerve
- 2 teaspoons ground cinnamon

1. Firstly, cream liquid monk fruit with butter until the mixture becomes fluffy. Sift in both types of flour.
2. Now, stir in the hazelnuts. Now, knead the mixture to form a dough; place in the refrigerator for about 35 minutes.
3. To finish, shape the prepared dough into bite-sized balls; arrange them on a baking dish; flatten the balls using the back of a spoon.
4. Mix granulated Swerve with ground cinnamon. Press your cookies in the cinnamon mixture until they are completely covered.
5. Bake the cookies for 20 minutes at 310 degrees.
6. Leave them to cool for about 10 minutes before transferring them to a wire rack. Bon appétit!

Per Serving: calories: 246 | fat: 23g | protein: 5g | carbs: 7g | net carbs: 3g | fiber: 4g

16.Walnut Butter Cookie

Prep Time:40 m | **Cook time:**15 m | **Serves:** 8

- ½ cup walnuts, ground
- ½ cup coconut flour
- 1 cup almond flour
- ¾ cup Swerve
- 1 stick butter, room temperature
- 2 tablespoons rum
- ½ teaspoon pure vanilla extract
- ½ teaspoon pure almond extract

1. In a mixing dish, beat the butter with Swerve, vanilla, and almond extract until light and fluffy. Then, throw in the flour and ground walnuts; add in rum.
2. Continue mixing until it forms a soft dough. Cover and place in the refrigerator for 20 minutes. In the meantime, preheat the Air Fryer to 330 degrees F (166ºC).
3. Roll the dough into small cookies, place them on the Air Fryer cake pan; gently press each cookie using a spoon.
4. Bake butter cookies for 15 minutes in the preheated Air Fryer. Bon appétit!

Per Serving: calories: 228 | fat: 22g | protein: 4g | carbs: 4g | net carbs: 2g | fiber: 2g

17.Buttery Almond Fruit Cookie

Prep Time:50 m | **Cook time:**13 m | **Serves:** 8

- ½ cup slivered almonds
- 1 stick butter, room temperature
- 4 ounces (113 g) monk fruit
- 2/3 cup blanched almond flour
- 1/3 cup coconut flour
- 1/3 teaspoon ground cloves
- 1 tablespoon ginger powder
- ¾ teaspoon pure vanilla extract

1. In a mixing dish, beat the monk fruit, butter, vanilla extract, ground cloves, and ginger until light and fluffy. Then, throw in the coconut flour, almond flour, and slivered almonds.
2. Continue mixing until it forms a soft dough. Cover and place in the refrigerator for 35 minutes. Meanwhile, preheat the Air Fryer to 315 degrees F (157ºC).
3. Roll dough into small cookies and place them on the Air Fryer cake pan; gently press each cookie using the back of a spoon.
4. Bake these butter cookies for 13 minutes. Bon appétit!

Per Serving: calories: 199 | fat: 19g | protein: 3g | carbs: 4g | net carbs: 2g | fiber: 2g

18.Butter and Chocolate Chip Cookie

Prep time: 20 m | **Cook time:** 11 m | **Serves:** 8

- 1 stick butter, at room temperature
- 1¼ cups Swerve
- ¼ cup chunky peanut butter
- 1 teaspoon vanilla paste
- 1 fine almond flour ²/₃ cup coconut flour
- ¹/₃ cup cocoa powder, unsweetened 1 ½ teaspoons baking powder
- ¼ teaspoon ground cinnamon
- ¼ teaspoon ginger
- ½ cup chocolate chips, unsweetened

1. In a mixing dish, beat the butter and Swerve until creamy and uniform. Stir in the peanut butter and vanilla.
2. In another mixing dish, thoroughly combine the flour, cocoa powder, baking powder, cinnamon, and ginger.
3. Add the flour mixture to the peanut butter mixture; mix to combine well. Afterward, fold in the chocolate chips.
4. Drop by large spoonfuls onto a parchment-lined Air Fryer basket. Bake at 365 degrees F (185°C) for 11 minutes or until golden brown on the top. Bon appétit!

Per Serving: calories: 303 | fat: 28g | protein: 6g | carbs: 10g | net carbs: 5g | fiber: 5g

19.Blueberry Cream Flan

Prep Time:30 m | **Cook time:**25 m | **Serves:** 6

- ¾ cup extra-fine almond flour
- 1 cup fresh blueberries ½ cup coconut cream
- ¾ cup coconut milk
- 3 eggs, whisked
- ½ cup Swerve
- ½ teaspoon baking soda
- ½ teaspoon baking powder
- ⅓ teaspoon ground cinnamon
- ½ teaspoon ginger
- ¼ teaspoon grated nutmeg

1. Lightly grease 2 mini pie pans using a nonstick cooking spray. Lay the blueberries on the bottom of the pie pans.
2. In a saucepan that is preheated over a moderate flame, warm the cream and coconut milk until thoroughly heated.
3. Remove the pan from the heat; mix in the flour along with baking soda and baking powder.
4. In a medium-sized mixing bowl, whip the eggs, Swerve, and spices; whip until the mixture is creamy.
5. Add the creamy milk mixture. Carefully spread this mixture over the fruits.
6. Bake at 320 degrees (160ºC) for about 25 minutes.

Per Serving: calories: 250 | fat: 22g | protein: 7g | carbs: 9g | net carbs: 6g | fiber: 3g

20.Air Fried Muffin

Prep Time:5 m | **Cook time:**25 m | **Serves:** 5

- ½ cup coconut flour
- 2 tablespoons cocoa powder
- 3 tablespoons erythritol
- 1 teaspoon baking powder
- 2 tablespoons coconut oil
- 2 eggs, beaten
- ½ cup coconut shred

1. In the mixing bowl, mix all ingredients.
2. Then, pour the mixture into the molds of the muffin and transfer it to the air fryer basket.
3. Cook the muffins at 350F (180ºC) for 25 minutes.

Per Serving: calories: 206 | fat: 16g | protein: 4g | carbs: 13g | net carbs: 6g | fiber: 7g

21.Homemade Muffin

Prep Time:10 m | **Cook time:**10 m | **Serves:** 5

- 5 tablespoons coconut oil, softened
- 1 egg, beaten
- 1 teaspoon vanilla extract
- 1 tablespoon poppy seeds
- 1 teaspoon baking powder
- 2 tablespoons erythritol
- 1 cup coconut flour

1. In the mixing bowl, mix coconut oil with egg, vanilla extract, poppy seeds, baking powder, erythritol, and coconut flour.
2. When the mixture is homogenous, pour it into the muffin molds and transfer it to the air fryer basket.
3. Cook the muffins for 10 minutes at 365F (185ºC).

Per Serving: calories: 239 | fat: 17g | protein: 5g | carbs: 17g | net carbs: 7g | fiber: 10g

22.Creamy Pecan Bar

Prep Time:5 m | **Cook time:**40 m | **Serves:** 12

- 2 cups coconut flour
- 5 tablespoons erythritol
- 4 tablespoons coconut oil, softened
- ½ cup heavy cream
- 1 egg, beaten
- 4 pecans, chopped

1. Mix coconut flour, erythritol, coconut oil, heavy cream, and egg.
2. Pour the batter into the air fryer basket and flatten well.
3. Top the mixture with pecans and cook the meal at 350F (180ºC) for 40 minutes.
4. Cut the cooked meal into the bars.

Per Serving: calories: 174 | fat: 12g | protein: 4g | carbs: 14g | net carbs: 5g | fiber: 9g

23.Lime Bar

Prep time: 10 m | **Cook time:**35 m | **Serves:** 10

- 3 tablespoons coconut oil, melted
- 3 tablespoons Splenda
- 1½ cup coconut flour
- 3 eggs, beaten
- 1 teaspoon lime zest, grated
- 3 tablespoons lime juice

1. Cover the air fryer basket bottom with baking paper.
2. Then, in the mixing bowl, mix Splenda with coconut flour, eggs, lime zest, and lime juice.
3. Pour the mixture into the air fryer basket and flatten gently.
4. Cook the meal at 350F (180ºC) for 35 minutes.
5. Then cool the cooked meal a little and cut it into bars.

Per Serving: calories: 144 | fat: 7g | protein: 4g | carbs: 16g | net carbs: 8g | fiber: 7g

24.Macadamia Bar

Prep time: 15 m | **Cook time:** 30 m | **Serves:** 10

- 3 tablespoons butter, softened
- 1 teaspoon baking powder
- 1 teaspoon apple cider vinegar
- 1.5 cup coconut flour
- 3 tablespoons Swerve
- 1 teaspoon vanilla extract
- 2 eggs, beaten
- 2 oz macadamia nuts, chopped
- Cooking spray

1. Spray the air fryer basket with cooking spray.
2. Then mix all remaining ingredients in the mixing bowl and stir until you get a homogenous mixture.
3. Pour the mixture in the air fryer basket and cook at 345F (174ºC) for 30 minutes.
4. When the mixture is cooked, cut it into bars and transfer it to the serving plates.

Per Serving: calories: 158 | fat: 10g | protein: 4g | carbs: 13g | net carbs: 5g | fiber: 8g

25.Creamy Vanilla Scones

Prep Time:20 m | **Cook time:**10 m | **Serves:** 6

- 4 oz coconut flour
- ½ teaspoon baking powder
- 1 teaspoon apple cider vinegar
- 2 teaspoons mascarpone
- ¼ cup heavy cream
- 1 teaspoon vanilla extract
- 1 tablespoon erythritol
- Cooking spray

1. In the mixing bowl, mix coconut flour with baking powder, apple cider vinegar, mascarpone, heavy cream, vanilla extract, and erythritol.
2. Knead the dough and cut it into scones.
3. Then, put them in the air fryer basket and sprinkle them with cooking spray.
4. Cook the vanilla scones at 365F (185ºC) for 10 minutes.

Per Serving: calories: 104 | fat: 4g | protein: 3g | carbs: 14g | net carbs: 6g | fiber: 8g

26.Homemade Mint Pie

Prep Time:15 m | **Cook time:**25 m | **Serves:** 2

- 1 tablespoon instant coffee
- 2 tablespoons almond butter, softened
- 2 tablespoons erythritol
- 1 teaspoon dried mint
- 3 eggs, beaten
- 1 teaspoon spearmint, dried
- 4 teaspoons coconut flour
- Cooking spray

1. Spray the air fryer basket with cooking spray.
2. Then mix all ingredients in the mixer bowl.
3. When you get a smooth mixture, transfer it to the air fryer basket. Flatten it gently.
4. Cook the pie at 365F (185ºC) for 25 minutes.

Per Serving: calories: 313 | fat: 19g | protein: 16g | carbs: 20g | net carbs: 8g | fiber: 12g

27.Cheese Keto Balls

Prep Time:15 m | **Cook time:**4 m | **Serves:** 10

- 2 eggs, beaten
- 1 teaspoon coconut oil, melted
- 9 oz coconut flour
- 5 oz provolone cheese, shredded
- 2 tablespoons erythritol
- 1 teaspoon baking powder
- ¼ teaspoon ground coriander Cooking spray

1. Mix eggs with coconut oil, coconut flour, Provolone cheese, erythritol, baking powder, and ground cinnamon.
2. Make the balls and put them in the air fryer basket.
3. Sprinkle the balls with cooking spray and cook at 400F (205ºC) for 4 minutes.

Per Serving: calories: 176 | fat: 7g | protein: 8g | carbs: 19g | net carbs: 8g | fiber: 11g

28.Pecan Butter Cookie

Prep Time:5 m | **Cook time:**24 m | **Makes** 12 cookies

- 1 cup chopped pecans
- ½ cup salted butter, melted
- ½ cup coconut flour
- ¾ cup erythritol, divided
- 1 teaspoon vanilla extract

1. In a food processor, blend pecans, butter, flour, ½ cup erythritol, and vanilla for 1 minute until a dough forms.
2. Form dough into twelve individual cookie balls, about 1 tablespoon each.
3. Cut three pieces of parchment to fit the air fryer basket. Place four cookies on each ungreased parchment and place one parchment piece with cookies into the air fryer basket. Adjust air fryer temperature to 325°F (163°C) and set the timer for 8 minutes. Repeat cooking with remaining batches.
4. When the timer goes off, allow cookies to cool for 5 minutes on a large serving plate until cool enough to handle. While still warm, dust cookies with remaining erythritol. Allow cooling completely, about 15 minutes, before serving.

Per Serving: calories: 151 | fat: 14g | protein: 2g | carbs: 13g | net carbs: 10g | fiber: 3g

29.Golden Doughnut Holes

Prep time: 10 m | **Cook time:**6 m | **Makes** 20 doughnut holes

- 1 cup blanched finely ground almond flour
- ½ cup low-carb vanilla protein powder
- ½ cup granular erythritol
- ¼ cup unsweetened cocoa powder ½ teaspoon baking powder
- 2 large eggs, whisked
- ½ teaspoon vanilla extract

1. Mix all ingredients in a large bowl until a soft dough forms. Separate and roll dough into twenty balls, about 2 tablespoons each.
2. Cut a piece of parchment to fit your air fryer basket. Working in batches if needed, place doughnut holes into air fryer basket on ungreased parchment. Adjust the temperature to 380°F (193ºC) and set the timer for 6 minutes, flipping doughnut holes halfway through cooking. Doughnut holes will be golden and firm when done. Let cool completely before serving, about 10 minutes.

Per Serving: calories: 103 | fat: 7g | protein: 8g | carbs: 13g | net carbs: 11g | fiber: 2g

30.Chocolate Chips Soufflés

Prep Time:5 m | **Cook time:**15 m | **Serves:** 2

- 2 large eggs, whites, and yolks separated
- 1 teaspoon vanilla extract
- 2 ounces (57 g) low-carb chocolate chips
- 2 teaspoons coconut oil, melted

1. In a medium bowl, beat egg whites until stiff peaks form, about 2 minutes. Set aside. In a separate medium bowl, whisk egg yolks and vanilla together. Set aside.
2. In a separate medium microwave-safe bowl, place chocolate chips and drizzle with coconut oil. Microwave on high for 20 seconds, then stir and continue cooking in 10-second increments until melted, careful not to overheat the chocolate. Let cool for 1 minute.
3. Slowly pour melted chocolate into egg yolks and whisk until smooth. Then, slowly begin adding egg white mixture to chocolate mixture, about ¼ cup at a time, folding in gently.
4. Pour mixture into two 4-inch ramekins greased with cooking spray. Place ramekins into air fryer basket. Adjust the temperature to 400°F (205ºC) and set the timer for 15 minutes. Soufflés will puff up while cooking and deflate a little once cooled. The center will be set when done. Let cool for 10 minutes, then serve warm.

Per Serving: calories: 217 | fat: 18g | protein: 8g | carbs: 19g | net carbs: 11g | fiber: 8g

31.Creamy Strawberry Pecan Pie

Prep time: 15 m | **Cook time:**10 m | **Serves:** 6

- 1½ cups whole shelled pecans
- 1 tablespoon unsalted butter, softened
- 1 cup heavy whipping cream
- 12 medium fresh strawberries, hulled
- 2 tablespoons sour cream

1. Place pecans and butter into a food processor and pulse ten times until a dough forms. Press dough into the bottom of an ungreased 6-inch round nonstick baking dish.
2. Place dish into air fryer basket. Adjust the temperature to 320°F (160°C) and set the timer for 10 minutes. The crust will be firm and golden when done. Let cool for 20 minutes.
3. In a large bowl, whisk the cream until fluffy and doubled in size, about 2 minutes.
4. In a separate large bowl, mash strawberries until mostly liquid. Fold strawberries and sour cream into whipped cream.
5. Spoon mixture into cooled crust, cover, and place into the refrigerator for at least 30 minutes to set. Serve chilled.

Per Serving: calories: 340 | fat: 33g | protein: 3g | carbs: 7g | net carbs: 4g | fiber: 3g

32.Chocolate Chip Cookie Cake

Prep Time:5 m | **Cook time:**15 m | **Serves:** 8

- 4 tablespoons salted butter, melted
- ⅓ cup granular brown erythritol
- 1 large egg
- ½ teaspoon vanilla extract
- 1 cup blanched finely ground almond flour
- ½ teaspoon baking powder
- ¼ cup low-carb chocolate chips

1. In a large bowl, whisk together butter, erythritol, egg, and vanilla. Add flour and baking powder, and stir until combined.
2. Fold in chocolate chips, then spoon batter into an ungreased 6-inch round nonstick baking dish.
3. Place dish into air fryer basket. Adjust the temperature to 300°F (150ºC) and set the timer for 15 minutes. When edges are browned, a cookie cake will be made.

Per Serving: calories: 170 | fat: 16g | protein: 4g | carbs: 15g | net carbs: 11g | fiber: 4g

33.Homemade Pretzels

Prep Time:10 m | **Cook time:**10 m | **Serves:** 6

- 1½ cups shredded Mozzarella cheese
- 1 cup blanched finely ground almond flour
- 2 tablespoons salted butter, melted, divided
- ¼ cup granular erythritol, divided
- 1 teaspoon ground cinnamon

1. Place Mozzarella, flour, 1 tablespoon butter, and 2 tablespoons erythritol in a large microwave-safe bowl. Microwave on high for 45 seconds, then stir with a fork until smooth dough ball forms.
2. Separate dough into six equal sections. Gently roll each section into a 12 -inch rope, then fold into a pretzel shape.
3. Place pretzels into an ungreased air fryer basket. Adjust the temperature to 370°F (188ºC) and set the timer for 8 minutes, turning pretzels halfway through cooking.
4. In a small bowl, combine the remaining butter, remaining erythritol, and cinnamon. Brush ½ mixture on both sides of pretzels.
5. Place pretzels back into the air fryer and cook an additional 2 minutes at 370°F (188ºC).
6. Transfer pretzels to a large plate. Brush on both sides with the remaining butter mixture, then let cool 5 minutes before serving.

Per Serving: calories: 223 | fat: 19g | protein: 11g | carbs: 13g | net carbs: 11g | fiber: 2g

34.Pecan Chocolate Brownies

Prep Time:10 m | **Cook time:** 20 m | **Serves:** 6

- ½ cup blanched finely ground almond flour
- ½ cup powdered erythritol
- 2 tablespoons unsweetened cocoa powder ½ teaspoon baking powder
- ¼ cup unsalted butter softened
- 1 large egg
- ¼ cup chopped pecans
- ¼ cup low-carb, sugar-free chocolate chips

1. In a large bowl, mix almond flour, erythritol, cocoa powder, and baking powder. Stir in butter and egg.
2. Fold in pecans and chocolate chips. Scoop mixture into 6 -inch round baking pan. Place pan into the air fryer basket.
3. Adjust the temperature to 300°F (150ºC) and set the timer for 20 minutes.
4. When fully cooked, a toothpick inserted in the center will come out clean. Allow 20 minutes to fully cool and firm up.

Per Serving: calories: 215 | fat: 18g | protein: 4g | carbs: 22g | net carbs: 19g | fiber: 3g

35.Butter Cheesecake

Prep Time:20 m | **Cook time:**35 m | **Serves:** 6

- ½ cup blanched finely ground almond flour
- 1 cup powdered erythritol, divided
- 2 tablespoons unsweetened cocoa powder
- ½ teaspoon baking powder
- ¼ cup unsalted butter softened
- 2 large eggs, divided
- 8 ounces (227 g) full-fat cream cheese, softened
- ¼ cup heavy whipping cream
- 1 teaspoon vanilla extract
- 2 tablespoons no-sugar-added peanut butter

1. In a large bowl, mix almond flour, ½ cup erythritol, cocoa powder, and baking powder. Stir in butter and one egg.
2 Scoop mixture into 6-inch round baking pan. Place pan into the air fryer basket.
3. Adjust the temperature to 300°F (150ºC) and set the timer for 20 minutes.
4. When fully cooked, a toothpick inserted in the center will come out clean. Allow 20 minutes to fully cool and firm up.
5. In a large bowl, beat cream cheese, remaining ½ cup erythritol, heavy cream, vanilla, peanut butter, and remaining egg until fluffy.
6. Pour mixture over cooled brownies. Place pan back into the air fryer basket.
7. Adjust the temperature to 300°F (150ºC) and set the timer for 15 minutes.
8. Cheesecake will be slightly browned and mostly firm with a slight jiggle when done. Allow to cool, then refrigerate 2 hours before serving.

Per Serving: calories: 347 | fat: 30g | protein: 8g | carbs: 30g | net carbs: 28g | fiber: 2g

36.Golden Cheese Cookie

Prep Time:10 m | **Cook time:**7 m | **Serves:** 6

- ½ cup blanched finely ground almond flour
- ½ cup powdered erythritol, divided
- 2 tablespoons butter, softened
- 1 large egg
- ½ teaspoon unflavored gelatin
- ½ teaspoon baking powder
- ½ teaspoon vanilla extract
- ½ teaspoon pumpkin pie spice
- 2 tablespoons pure pumpkin purée
- ½ teaspoon ground cinnamon, divided
- ¼ cup low-carb, sugar-free chocolate chips
- 3 ounces (85 g) full-fat cream cheese, softened

1. In a large bowl, mix almond flour and ¼ cup erythritol. Stir in butter, egg, and gelatin until combined.
2. Stir in baking powder, vanilla, pumpkin pie spice, pumpkin purée, and ¼ teaspoon cinnamon, then fold in chocolate chips.
3. pour batter into a 6-inch round baking pan. Place pan into the air fryer basket.
4. Adjust the temperature to 300°F (150°C) and set the timer for 7 minutes.
5. When fully cooked, the top will be golden brown, and a toothpick inserted in the center will come out clean. Let cool for at least 20 minutes.
6. Make the frosting: mix cream cheese, remaining ¼ teaspoon cinnamon and remaining ¼ cup erythritol in a large bowl. Using an electric mixer, beat until it becomes fluffy. Spread onto the cooled cookie. Garnish with additional cinnamon if desired.

Per Serving: calories: 199 | fat: 16g | protein: 5g | carbs: 22g | net carbs: 20g | fiber: 2g

37.Toasted Coconut Flakes

Prep Time:5 m | **Cook time:**3 m | **Serves:** 4

- 1 cup unsweetened coconut flakes
- 2 teaspoons coconut oil
- ¼ cup granular erythritol ⅛ teaspoon salt

1. Toss coconut flakes and oil in a large bowl until coated. Sprinkle with erythritol and salt.
2. Place coconut flakes into the air fryer basket.
3. Adjust the temperature to 300°F (150ºC) and set the timer for 3 minutes.
4. Toss the flakes when 1 minute remains. Add an extra minute if you would like a more golden coconut flake.
5. Store in an airtight container for up to 3 days.

Per Serving: calories: 165 | fat: 15g | protein: 1g | carbs: 20g | net carbs: 17g | fiber: 3g

38.Cheesy Cream Cake

Prep Time:10 m | **Cook time:**25 m | **Serves:** 6

- 1 cup blanched finely ground almond flour
- ¼ cup salted butter, melted ½ cup granular erythritol
- 1 teaspoon vanilla extract
- 1 teaspoon baking powder ½ cup full-fat sour cream
- 1 ounce (28 g) full-fat cream cheese, softened 2 large eggs

1. In a large bowl, mix almond flour, butter, and erythritol.

2. Add in vanilla, baking powder, sour cream, and cream cheese and mix until well combined. Add eggs and mix.

3. Pour batter into a 6-inch round baking pan. Place pan into the air fryer basket.

4. Adjust the temperature to 300°F (150ºC) and set the timer for 25 minutes.

5. When the cake is made, a toothpick inserted in the center will come out clean. The center should not feel wet. Allow it to cool completely, or the cake will crumble when moved.

Per Serving: calories: 253 | fat: 22g | protein: 7g | carbs: 25g | net carbs: 23g | fiber: 2g

39.Cheese Monkey Bread

Prep Time:15 m | **Cook time:**12 m | **Serves:** 6

- ½ cup blanched finely ground almond flour
- ½ cup low-carb vanilla protein powder
- ¾ cup granular erythritol, divided ½ teaspoon baking powder
- 8 tablespoons salted butter, melted and divided 1 ounce (28 g) full-fat cream cheese, softened 1 large egg
- ¼ cup heavy whipping cream ½ teaspoon vanilla extract

1. In a large bowl, combine almond flour, protein powder, ½ cup erythritol, baking powder, 5 tablespoons butter, cream cheese, and egg. A soft, sticky dough will form.
2. Place the dough in the freezer for 20 minutes. It will be firm enough to roll into balls. Wet your hands with warm water and roll into twelve balls. Place the balls into a 6-inch round baking dish.
3. In a medium skillet over medium heat, melt the remaining butter with remaining erythritol. Lower the heat and continue stirring until the mixture turns golden, then add cream and vanilla. Remove from heat and allow it to thicken for a few minutes while you continue to stir.
4. While the mixture cools, place the baking dish into the air fryer basket.
5. Adjust the temperature to 320°F (160ºC) and set the timer for 6 minutes.
6. When the timer beeps, flip the monkey brvad over onto a plate and slide it back into the baking pan. Cook an additional 4 minutes until all the tops are brown.
7. Pour the caramel sauce over the monkey bread and cook an additional 2 minutes. Let cool completely before serving.

Per Serving: calories: 322 | fat: 24g | protein: 20g | carbs: 34g | net carbs: 32g | fiber: 2g

40.Cheesy Cream Puffs

Prep Time:15 m | **Cook time:**6 m | **Makes** 8 puffs

- ½ cup blanched finely ground almond flour
- ½ cup low-carb vanilla protein powder
- ½ cup granular erythritol
- ½ teaspoon baking powder
- 1 large egg
- 5 tablespoons unsalted butter, melted
- 2 ounces (57 g) full-fat cream cheese
- ¼ cup powdered erythritol
- ¼ teaspoon ground cinnamon
- 2 tablespoons heavy whipping cream
- ½ teaspoon vanilla extract

1. Mix almond flour, protein powder, granular erythritol, baking powder, egg, and butter in a large bowl until a soft dough forms.
2. Place the dough in the freezer for 20 minutes. Wet your hands with water and roll the dough into eight balls.
3. Cut a piece of parchment to fit your air fryer basket. Working in batches as necessary, place the dough balls into the air fryer basket on top of the parchment.
4. Adjust the temperature to 380°F (193ºC) and set the timer for 6 minutes.
5. Flip cream puffs halfway through the cooking time.
6. When the timer beeps, remove the puffs and allow them to cool.
7. In a medium bowl, beat the cream cheese, powdered erythritol, cinnamon, cream, and vanilla until fluffy.
8. Place the mixture into a pastry bag or a storage bag with the end snipped. Cut a small hole in the bottom of each puff and fill with some of the cream mixtures.
9. Store in an airtight container for up to 2 days in the refrigerator.

Per Serving: calories: 178 | fat: 12g | protein: 15g | carbs: 22g | net carbs: 21g | fiber: 1g

41.Zucchini Bread

Prep Time:10 m | **Cook time:**40 m | **Serves:** 12

- 2 cups coconut flour
- 2 teaspoons baking powder
- ¾ cup erythritol
- ½ cup coconut oil, melted
- 1 teaspoon apple cider vinegar
- 1 teaspoon vanilla extract
- 3 eggs, beaten
- 1 zucchini, grated
- 1 teaspoon ground cinnamon

1. In the mixing bowl, mix coconut flour with baking powder, erythritol, coconut oil, apple cider vinegar, vanilla extract, eggs, zucchini, and ground cinnamon
2. Transfer the mixture to the air fryer basket and flatten it in the bread's shape.
3. Cook the bread at 350F (180ºC) for 40 minutes.

Per Serving: calories: 179 | fat: 12g | protein: 4g | carbs: 15g | net carbs: 7g | fiber: 8g

42.Orange Cinnamon Cookies

Prep Time:15 m | **Cook Time:** 24 m | **Servings:**10

- 3 tablespoons cream cheese
- 3 tablespoons Erythritol
- 1 teaspoon vanilla extract
- ½ teaspoon ground cinnamon
- 1 egg, beaten
- 1 cup almond flour
- ½ teaspoon baking powder
- 1 teaspoon butter, softened
- ½ teaspoon orange zest, grated

Put the cream cheese and Erythritol in the bowl. Add vanilla extract, ground cinnamon, and almond flour. Stir the mixture with the help of the spoon until homogenous. Then add egg, almond flour, baking powder, and butter. Add orange zest and stir the mass until homogenous. Then knead it with the help of the fingertips. Roll up the dough with the help of the rolling pin. Then make the cookies with the help of the cookie cutter. Preheat the air fryer to 365F. Line the air fryer basket with baking paper. Put the cookies on the baking paper and cook them for 8 minutes. The time of cooking depends on the cooking size.

Per Serving: calories 38, fat 3.3, fiber 0.4, carbs 1, protein 1.4

43.Mini Almond Cakes

Prep Time:10 m | **Cook Time:** 20 m | **Servings:**4

- 3 ounces dark chocolate, melted
- ¼ cup coconut oil, melted
- 2 tablespoons swerve
- 2 eggs, whisked
- ¼ teaspoon vanilla extract
- 1 tablespoon almond flour
- Cooking spray

In a bowl, combine all the ingredients except the cooking spray and whisk well. Divide this into 4 ramekins greased with cooking spray, put them in the fryer, and cook at 360 degrees F for 20 minutes. Serve warm.

Per Serving: calories 161, fat 12, fiber 1, carbs 4, protein 7

44.Chia Bites

Prep Time:15 m | **Cook Time:** 8 m | **Servings:** 2

- ½ scoop of protein powder
- 1 egg, beaten
- 3 tablespoons almond flour
- 1 oz hazelnuts, grinded
- 1 tablespoon flax meal
- 1 teaspoon Splenda
- 1 teaspoon butter, softened
- 1 teaspoon chia seeds, dried
- ¼ teaspoon ground clove

In the mixing bowl, mix up protein powder, almond flour, ground hazelnuts, flax meal, chia seeds, ground clove, and Splenda. Then add egg and butter and stir it with the spoon's help until you get a homogenous mixture. Cut the mixture into pieces and make 2 bites of any shape with the help of the fingertips. Preheat the air fryer to 365F. Line the air fryer basket with baking paper and put the protein bites inside. Cook them for 8 minutes.

Per Serving: calories 433, fat 35.5, fiber 7, carbs 15.6, protein 20.2

45.Espresso Cinnamon Cookies

Prep Time:5 m | **Cook Time:** 15 m | **Servings:** 12

- 8 tablespoons ghee, melted
- 1 cup almond flour
- ¼ cup brewed espresso
- ¼ cup swerve
- ½ tablespoon cinnamon powder
- 2 teaspoons baking powder
- 2 eggs, whisked

In a bowl, mix all the ingredients and whisk well. Spread medium balls on a cookie sheet lined with parchment paper, flatten them, put the cookie sheet in your air fryer and cook at 350 degrees F for 15 minutes. Serve the cookies cold.

Per Serving: calories 134, fat 12, fiber 2, carbs 4, protein 2

46.Turmeric Almond Pie

Prep Time:20 m | **Cook Time:** 35 m | **Servings:**4

- 4 eggs, beaten
- 1 tablespoon poppy seeds
- 1 teaspoon ground turmeric
- 1 teaspoon vanilla extract
- 1 teaspoon baking powder
- 1 teaspoon lemon juice
- 1 cup almond flour
- 2 tablespoons heavy cream
- ¼ cup Erythritol
- 1 teaspoon avocado oil

Put the eggs in the bowl. Add vanilla extract, baking powder, lemon juice, almond flour, heavy cream, and Erythritol. Then add avocado oil and poppy seeds. Add turmeric. With the help of the immersion blender, blend the pie batter until it is smooth. Line the air fryer cake mold with baking paper. Pour the pie batter into the cake mold. Flatten the pie surface with the help of the spatula if needed. Then preheat the air fryer to 365F. Put the cake mold in the air fryer and cook the pie for 35 minutes. When the pie is cooked, cool it completely and remove it from the cake mold. Cut the cooked pie into the servings.

Per Serving: calories 149, fat 11.9, fiber 1.2, carbs 3.8, protein 7.7

47.Sponge Cake

Prep Time:5 m | **Cook Time:** 30 m | **Servings:** 8

- 1 cup ricotta, soft
- 1/3 swerve
- 3 eggs, whisked
- 1 cup almond flour
- 7 tablespoons ghee, melted
- 1 teaspoon baking powder
- Cooking spray

In a bowl, combine all the ingredients except the cooking spray and stir them very well. Grease a cake pan that fits the air fryer with the cooking spray and pour the cake mix inside. Put the pan in the fryer and cook at 350 degrees F for 30 minutes. Cool the cake down, slice, and serve.

Per Serving: calories 210, fat 12, fiber 3, carbs 6, protein 9

48.Cinnamon and Butter Pancakes

Prep Time:10 m | **Cook Time:** 12 m | **Servings:** 2

- 1 teaspoon ground cinnamon
- 2 teaspoons butter, softened
- 1 teaspoon baking powder
- ½ teaspoon lemon juice
- ½ teaspoon vanilla extract
- ¼ cup heavy cream
- 4 tablespoons almond flour
- 2 teaspoons Erythritol

Preheat the air fryer to 325F. Take 2 small cake molds and line them with baking paper. After this, mix up ground cinnamon, butter, baking powder, lemon juice, vanilla extract, heavy cream, almond flour, and Erythritol in the mixing bowl. Stir the mixture until it is smooth. Then pour the mixture into the prepared cake molds. Put the first cake mold in the air fryer and cook the pancake for 6 minutes. Then check if the pancake is cooked (it should have light brown color) and remove it from the air fryer. Repeat the same steps with the second pancake. It is recommended to serve the pancakes warm or hot.

Per Serving: calories 414, fat 37.4, fiber 6.7, carbs 14.7, protein 12.4

49.Strawberry Cups

Prep Time:5 m | **Cook Time:** 10 m | **Servings:** 8

- 16 strawberries, halved
- 2 tablespoons coconut oil
- 2 cups chocolate chips, melted

In a pan that fits your air fryer, mix the strawberries with the oil and the melted chocolate chips, toss gently, put the pan in the air fryer, and cook at 340 degrees F for 10 minutes. Divide into cups and serve cold.

Per Serving: calories 162, fat 5, fiber 3, carbs 5, protein6

50.Cardamom Squares
Prep Time:15 m | **Cook Time:** 20 m | **Servings:** 4

- 4 tablespoons peanut butter
- 1 tablespoon peanut, chopped
- 1 teaspoon vanilla extract
- ½ cup coconut flour
- 1 tablespoon Erythritol
- ½ teaspoon ground cardamom

Put the peanut butter and peanut in the bowl. Add vanilla extract, coconut flour, and ground cardamom. Then add Erythritol and stir the mixture until homogenous. Preheat the air fryer to 330F. Line the air fryer basket with baking paper and pour the peanut butter mixture over it. Flatten it gently and cook for 20 minutes. Then remove the cooked mixture from the air fryer and cool it completely. Cut the dessert into squares.

Per Serving: calories 181, fat 11.7, fiber 7.2, carbs 12.8, protein 7.6

CPSIA information can be obtained
at www.ICGtesting.com
Printed in the USA
BVHW062017190321
602998BV00004B/44